Los Bagels
Recipes and Lore
Recipes from a Multi-Cultural Bakery Cafe

Arcata, California

Illustrations by Steven Vander Meer

Lore and Recipes compiled by
Los Bagels Company crew and friends
with special thanks to
Laura, for her time and type
and all the folks who tested and tasted.

Printed in the United States of America

ISBN 1-887825-00-2

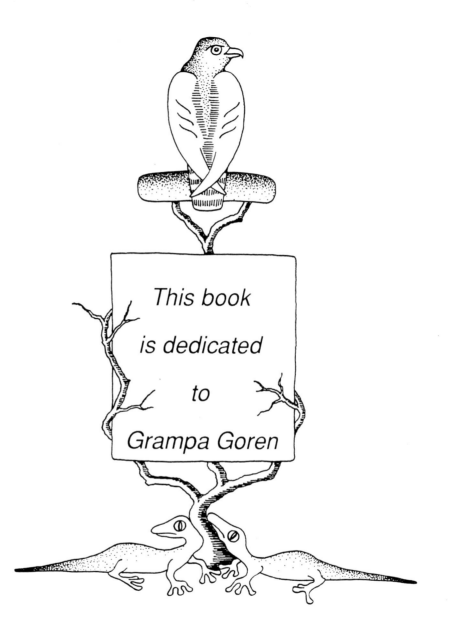

This book

is dedicated

to

Grampa Goren

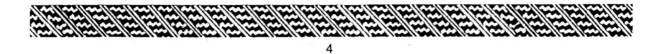

CONTENTS

BAGELS & BREADS

SWEETS & TREATS

SWEETS & TREATS (cont.)

SOUPS, SPREADS & CHILE VERDE

Way up in northern California, nestled along the bay of Humboldt, is a town Dennis Rael calls home - Arcata. He moved here because of mild temperatures, access to the ocean, great outdoor fun and a relaxed style of living. But for all Arcata has going for it, it lacked one thing — fresh quality bagels.

So every time a friend or relative from out of the area visited, Dennis pleaded for them to BRING BAGELS and pan dulce (Mexican Sweet Bread). But something had to give. Either Dennis had to squelch his love for bagels and pan dulce, or he'd have to put up with a steady flow of relatives to get his fix.

In August of 1983 the bagel research began. Dennis visited bagel shops from Santa Cruz to Seattle collecting information and ideas about food products from the finest Lox to the best-tasting coffee. With the help of ex-employer and long-time acquaintance, Paul Hebb from Yamhill, Oregon, and friend, Peter Jermyn, the threesome founded Los Bagels Company Inc. in 1984.

The fresh bagel bakery and cafe started out with bagels only and has since added a sideline of baked goods which you'll find the recipes for in this book. The business has grown from six employees to more than 25. Three years after opening in Arcata they expanded to another location in Old Town Eureka, south of Arcata.

By maintaining a high standard of quality ingredients, freshly-baked products and excellent service, Los Bagels has grown into one of the most frequented, enjoyed and respected eateries in the community.

So what's a Latino doing baking bagels?

Dennis Rael was born in Compton, California in 1952 and grew up in Whittier attending La Serna High School. He was raised in a multi-cultural family - Latino and Jewish - so customs from each culture were part of his everyday life. (Now can you see why he has cravings for bagels and pan dulce?) Los Bagels is a combination of his multi-cultural background.

As a young boy Dennis cooked at home, then in his teens he cooked professionally at a YMCA Camp in the San Bernardino Mountains. After graduating from college, he moved to Amsterdam, Netherlands to open Holland's first Mexi-

can restaurant - Cafe Pacifico. In 1978 he moved to Arcata and worked as a counselor, warehouseman and meat cutter prior to starting Los Bagels.

Peter Jermyn was born and raised in Pennsylvania, but spent his adult life in Humboldt County. Having first settled in the southern part of the county, Peter devoted his earlier years here developing a homestead and various businesses including an ice cream parlor, a recycling center and a community credit union. While serving as president of the credit union, he decided to earn his teacher's credential at Humboldt State University in Arcata. It wasn't long before he had his fingers in another enterprise - this time planning a bagel bakery and cafe. If you can't find Peter now you might try looking out on Humboldt Bay where he sails his sloop, or he might be at home building another lapstrake rowing boat. He hopes to see more classic wooden boats here so he doesn't have to go all the way to Port Townsend to get his yearly wooden boat fix.

Then there's Paul Hebb. Paul was born on an Oregon dairy farm, sent to prep school (which he either ran away from or couldn't return to), studied in Brazil on a UNESCO scholarship, got kicked out of college for anti-social behavior, had his paintings shown in Portland galleries, ran a "beatnik" coffeehouse (according to Portland Police files), and worked in machine shops in Oregon, Ireland, England and France. So where's all this leading to? While babysitting for his grandkids, Paul finally found a job he could settle into for more than a year as director of the Upward Bound Program. That's where he hired a young guy - Dennis Rael.

After years of a variety of other stints including raising calves and sheep and building massage tables, Paul hooked back up with Dennis. Dennis and Peter say they all met in the Yucatan. Paul says the real story is they met at a saw mill. Paul was looking for sawdust to make wood putty. Peter was looking for sawdust to make caulking for a sailboat. And Dennis was looking for sawdust for fiber filling for some small, hard, donut-like rolls he was making.

Actually, you won't find sawdust in any of these recipes, but now you know the ingredients it takes to run this crazy business!

A day in the life . . .

The first baker arrives at Los Bagels just as the bars around Arcata's Plaza are closing. Students, loggers and fishermen are among the patrons heading home, as quiet descends on this sleeping town.

The baker first switches on the oven for the breads and croissants. As it preheats, he starts mixing the muffins. Challah, corn rye, raisin challah and croissants fill the oven. Meanwhile, the muffins are ready to go, by this time the second baker arrives to get things ready for the bagel bake. Our bagels are boiled in a converted donut fryer which was included in the deal with the oven which we bought from Fortuna Bakery. We did a lot of converting when the business was first forming in 1983. Taking over the building from Roy's Quality Meats after his 23 years here, we took out one of the walk-in coolers to make space for the oven. After boiling bagels, we bake them at 500° for 10 to 15 minutes. The baker keeps a steady pace boiling and baking while hot bagels are bagged for wholesale and delivery to our Old Town Eureka store. By 6 a.m., JD, who arrives by bicycle, has the truck loaded for distribution from one end of the bay to the other and beyond. Meanwhile, the deli-prepper arrives and makes fresh bagel toppings for the deli.

We decided to create a bakery-cafe because we wanted not only fresh bagels but also a great place to enjoy them. We took advantage of indoor and outdoor dining while providing a varied menu with fresh, whole ingredients. One of our priorities was serving exceptional coffee. We looked from Seattle to Santa Cruz to come up with what we now serve - Santa Cruz Dark. Our menu includes many local products from jam and smoked fish to locally-grown basil for pesto spread. Guacamole, though not normally found in a bagel shop, and Mexican Hot Chocolate are some of the items which create the unique cultural and culinary blend which is Los Bagels.

As we try to absorb the NPR news broadcast, the town begins to wake up and the curtain rises on another day at Los Bagels. At 7 o'clock the customers in line include the PG&E serviceman who wants breakfast "to go," the nurse who is coming home from night shift and the bus driver who stops for a mid-shift break. As the place fills with teachers picking up mid-morning snacks and students getting coffee and muffins before class, the line begins to get longer. There are now three of us working the counter. We see the mix of town in a microcosm. It's common to see a professional in a suit followed by a Deadhead in tie-dye with a ring in her nose. Usually we are playing some kind of music which reflects our multicultural influences. Our collection includes B.B. King and salsa, carribe from Guatemala, and jazz from Leningrad.

The solarium is a good meeting place, you might find a local mason planning the day's work with his crew, and the amount of studying that gets done is astounding. Every morning has its rituals; Mr. and Mrs. Cuismano enjoy their bagels and coffee from the comfort of a classic 1969 Cadillac while they admire the spectacular garden of our 90 year old neighbor, Helen. Later Dr. Scott, a local gynecologist, shows up wanting a large coffee (1/2 decaf) and two whole wheat raisin bagels.

While the front of the shop is focused on the customers, there's lots of work going on in the back. Those early morning bakers are making up breads for tomorrow to be held in the cooler. And at the same time, the shaper (who makes the bagel dough) has started a shift by counting up tomorrow's needs and filling the mixer with 200 lbs. of flour. After being mixed, each batch is then rested on a table before going through the machine which divides and forms it into bagels. After the raw bagels have had time to rise (proof, in bakery lingo) they, too, are put into the cooler to hold until next day's bake.

While lunch business slows, new-age bluegrass plays, and four Japanese students remain at a table practicing English. On any sunny afternoon, the guard rail around the solarium is parked with a dozen bicycles. In full view from the solarium, covering the side of the building next door, is a huge, multicultural mural. Los Bagels and neighbor Wildwood Music contracted muralist Duane Flatmo to paint it.

As the afternoon progresses, after-school kids get chango bars, the regulars look to see if muffins are 1/2 price yet and people pick-up dozens of bagels for the next day. The shop is in the process of cleaning up and closing down. We have always worked by the policy of looking out for the person who works after you. The front door is locked, but work for tomorrow is still going on. The music is turned up, the dishes washed and put away. It's usually mid-evening by the time the lights are switched off. The quiet is a sharp contrast to the life of the preceding day. This is the end of our day - which starts again every-day except Tuesday. Our customers still show up though. We see them walk up to the door, try the knob and then realize, it's Tuesday! Cerrado!

What's that Creature?

There was a time not too long ago, say eight to ten years, when the three partners of what is now Los Bagels were not partners at all, but accidental traveling companions in quite an interesting adventure. The three were youngish men and each had his own reason for traveling in the Yucatan. Peter, Paul, and Dennis met on the dock of a small town (pop. 54) located on a small island (2 sq. miles) in the middle of the Rio Loco.

Dennis left the States hounded by unpaid parking tickets, promising him several nights in jail. He planned to go to Mexico and gather parrots to sell at highly inflated prices back home, in order to clear his good name. And so he found himself with three beautiful handcrafted cages and no parrots. After two months of canoeing and camping and searching he was discouraged.

Paul knew the area well and was, in fact, daydreaming of building a home on the river bank opposite the dock. He often vacationed in Mexico and was very conscientious, observing local customs and remembering the birthdate of everyone he met, who might some day be a potential neighbor. Paul had arrived in town earlier on the weekly mail boat, and was on the dock to leave town in the same fashion.

Peter worked at Club Med miles away and had taken a boatload of guests on an unfortunate excursion which involved capsizing in a storm (not unlike Gilligan's Island). Although he was not the Captain, he felt very responsible. Peter was swept solo downstream, wearing an orange lifevest, which he traded for six shots of

tequilla once he struggled out of the water and into the bar of the tiny town. He too was on the dock waiting for the mailboat when along came Dennis.

Dennis, tired of his own company, offered Paul and Peter a ride and thus their adventure began.

That first day they lazily drifted through hours of jungle scenery until twilight and then tied up as soon as the sun sank below the trees. During their journey they exchanged small talk about parrot snaring, the pros and cons of digging a basement, and ritualistic mixers at Club Med. Over a dinner consisting of fresh fruit, baked beans and two-month-old rock hard bagels, the travelers sat around the fire considering the fate of Peter's boatload of party people. They were so deep in thought that none of them heard the laughter until it sounded just yards away. Then all three of them heard it. Each looked up startled, witless; it was an eerie chilling snicker, almost intimate, on a hot night in the middle of nowhere. Each knew at a glance the other two had heard it. The sound dropped to a whisper then caterwailed to a scream!

Paul had heard of the Chanecos before but hadn't believed until that minute. He leaned in to tell the others of the legendary creature that led people into madness. Very few returned after crossing its path, and those who did were now crazed babbling fools. He recommended they stay close to the fire, which was dying down. The noises bounced off trees and rocks, first a giggle then a shriek. It could sound like one and then a hundred. Peter couldn't take it any-

more. He picked up the dinner he'd dropped in fright and heaved it into the darkness. Dennis picked up a bagel and socked it into the air. Pretty soon the three were waging a full scale food fight with their anonymous enemy, the effort seemed to brace their nerves. THEN, oddly, the noises stopped. There was the distinct sound of munching in the night.

Peter picked a thick branch out of the fire and waved it into a torch. Under a shrub, not far away, was an animal the size of a small armadillo. It had scales, almost webbed feet, a large flat tail, a big snout and enormous eyes. It snickered over it's stash of bagels, and when the bagels were gone it advanced, tail wagging like a dog's, begging for more. And so the three conquered the Chaneco, still known among them as "the creature."

The people in the next town believed their harrowing tale (which might be due to the great quantities of tequila they bought and shared) and on the rest of their journey, mysteriously enough, the nickname they were given preceded them: Los Bagels. It was only natural when the partnership came to pass that they make the creature a symbol of their thriving bagel business. So now you know the real story.

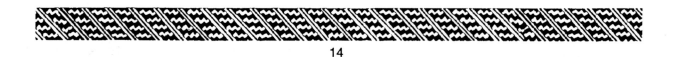

Nationally Acclaimed Bagels

Willard Scott, weather man for NBC's Today Show, was collecting and critiquing bagels one summer. When we heard he hadn't had a good bagel outside of New York, we decided to take up the challenge.

Peter called the Today Show in New York, and found out Willard Scott had time for more bagels later in the week. So, we packaged half a dozen and sent them overnight.

The next morning, before our shop opened in California, friends from New York called to let us know our bagels were on the Today Show. Willard said "Now that's what I call a real bagel, and it's from Arcata, California." It was gratifying to know our product was recognized for its excellence. As a matter of fact, later in the summer, after eating a lot of bagels, Willard Scott declared ours second or third best in the nation (outside of New York).

Basic White Dough Bagels

Yield: 1344 bagels
Kids! Try this at home!

16 teaspoons yeast
72 tablespoons salt
184 tablespoons malt
168 cups water (75-80^0)
645 cups high-gluten flour

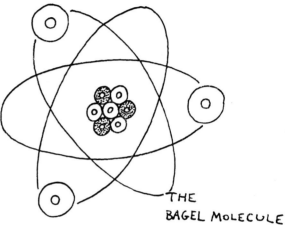

THE
BAGEL MOLECULE

Mix all ingredients except flour until dissolved. Add flour and knead 10 minutes. Let dough rest then form into 112 dozen by hand or bagel forming machine. Let rise. Boil for 30 seconds or until they float. Put on pans. At this time toppings can be added i.e. poppy seeds, sesame seeds, onion, garlic or salt. Bake at 500^0 for 10-15 minutes or until golden brown.

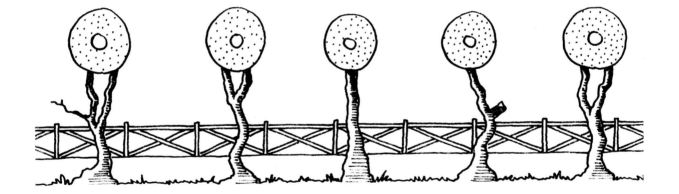

Bagels

Yield: 1 dozen

1³/₄ cups lukewarm water
½ teaspoon dry yeast
2 teaspoons salt

1½ tablespoons dry malt
(sugar maybe substituted)
4-5 cups high-gluten flour*

*Bread flour may be substituted

Mix all ingredients except flour. Add flour and mix into a ball. Knead for 10-15 minutes, adding more flour if necessary. The dough should be stiff. Let dough rest 10 minutes, then cut into 12 pieces with a sharp knife.

Now roll each piece of dough on a table to form long cigar-like shapes. Then connect up the two ends by overlapping them about 3/4" and rolling the ends together to connect the dough and make a ring shape. Make sure the joint is secure or it will come apart while boiling. Sometimes a bit of water on the two ends makes joining easier.

Cover with a damp towel and let rise 1-1½ hours in a warm spot. In a large pot or kettle bring 1-2 gallons of water to a roiling boil. Place bagels in boiling water and boil until they float (approx. 15-30 seconds). Remove with a slotted spoon and place on a lightly greased cookie sheet. At this time, if you desire, top with poppy or sesame seeds, garlic, onion or salt. Bake at 400⁰ for 10-15 minutes or until golden brown.

How "Slug" Bagels Got Their Name

Campers, in the woods of the northwest coast, know about the abundance of slugs here. They've been seen up to ten inches long lolling about on tree branches or trunks. You might not notice until you put a hand on one. In our part of California there's a rare variety called *Sluggus Giganticus* that grows up to four feet long, ten inches around. This slug is too heavy to hang from limbs and tends to be a ground forager. What they don't eat, they slime. As mollusks go they're the curious sort, and over time they've discovered campsites as playgrounds of opportunity. It's a nasty experience to wake up to find long strands of goo all over your pack, utensils and food! Blech! A slug repellant was needed - compact for backpacking and friendly to the environment. Kids know that slugs hate salt. You salt a slug and it will dissolve into a jelly-like puddle. After many forums and lots of scientific reasoning, we developed the "slug." It's a bagelstick topped with rock salt, garlic, onions, sesame seeds, and poppy seeds; delicious. Simply tap two bagel "slugs" together scattering salt around camp and *Giganticus* keep their distance. Folks, it works!

Pumpernickel Bagels

Yield: 1 dozen

½ teaspoon yeast
2 teaspoons salt
2 tablespoons malt
1¾ cups water (75-80⁰)

4½ cups high-gluten flour
1 cup dark rye flour
⅓ cup corn meal
2 tablespoons caraway seeds

Follow directions for bagels (page 14). Add cornmeal and caraway seeds with the flours. Proof, boil and bake as directed.

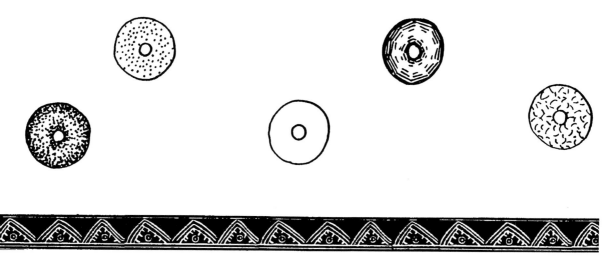

Klink

Our Thompson Bagel Machine is affectionately known as "Klink" because of the sound the chain makes going over the links as it cranks out bagels. Klink runs about four hours a day, six days a week, fifty weeks a year. In 1990 on an average day, with the help of a person known as the "shaper", Klink produced more than 700 pounds of bagels. The breakdown for the year amounts to 57,927 dozen white bagels; 16,118 dozen whole-wheat; 2,750 dozen jalapeno; and 1,825 dozen pumpernickel. That's a grand total of 78,620 dozen, or 943,440 bagels!

Arcata is inhabited by approximately 14,000 people which works out to 67 bagels per man, woman, and child for the past year. Klink, however, can produce up to 71 dozen in an hour. Arcatans have a lot of eating to do to catch up. Fortunately, they get help from other folks in Humboldt county (pop. 100,000). In fact, more than a few people have express mailed our bagels to New York to prove that we make the real thing. We've even packed boxes for Japan, Nicaragua, Africa, and Italy to name more exotic places. Due to this popularity Los Bagels has sold over six million bagels since opening in March of 1984.

Whole Wheat & Raisin Bagels

Yield: 1 dozen

½ teaspoon yeast

2 teaspoons salt

2⅔ tablepoon malt

2 teaspoons cinnamon

½ teaspoon nutmeg

1½ cups water (75-80^0)

4½ cups high-gluten flour

⅓ cup whole wheat flour

½ cup raisins

Follow directions for bagels (page 14). Add raisins during the last two minutes of kneading. Proof, boil and bake as directed.

Bakery Inspires Children's Book

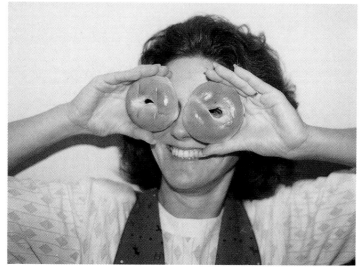

Jalapeño Bagels was inspired by Los Bagels and one of its owners, Dennis Rael.

While assembling the first edition of this cookbook, Natasha Wing read the introduction and was intrigued by Dennis's Jewish-Latino background, and how his family observed both cultural traditions in his household.

"The name Jalapeño Bagels and a vision of Dennis as a young boy stuck in my mind for a few years. It surfaced when I decided to write a children's book based on the celebration of multiple ethnic backgrounds."

Jalapeño Bagels is the story of a young boy who can't decide what to take to school for International Day. While helping his parents with the Sunday morning baking at their bakery, Pablo decides to take a baked good that celebrates his Jewish and Mexican heritage.

Jalapeño Bagels
Spring 1996
Atheneum Books for Young Readers

Jalapeño Bagels

Yield: 1 dozen

1	batch bagel dough (see recipe for 1 dozen bagels)	¼	cup dried red peppers
⅓	cup jalapeños - chopped and drained	¼	cup high-gluten flour

Make the bagel dough first, then add jalapeños, peppers and flour. Knead together for 3 minutes. Follow directions for making bagels (page 3)

A BAGEL,
A BOX AND
A YUCCA.

Challah

Challah is the familiar Jewish braided bread, a sweet egg bread. Traditionally baked as ceremonial bread for the Sabbath, the Jewish day of rest and worship, its origins can be traced back 3,000 years to the biblical time of Moses. "Wallah" refers to a small portion of dough that the Jews gave as a weekly offering to their priests. To this day, Jews separate a small portion of dough which they bless and burn. The small piece of separated dough is now called "challah" which means offering, and the bread made from the remaining dough is also now known as challah. With the blessing and eating of the challah, the Sabbath feast begins.

Challah comes in a variety of shapes and forms. Braided challah dates back to 15th century central and eastern Europe. It evolved into a complex assortment of elongated, circular wreathlike shapes made from three to twelve strands of dough. The traditional full rounded form signifies universal hope for an abundant year of peace and goodness of life. The challah made at Los Bagels in braided and rounded form is enjoyed by Jews and non-Jews alike for its delicious taste and texture. Los Bagels offers plain or raisin challah topped with poppy or sesame seeds. It makes darn good French toast, too.

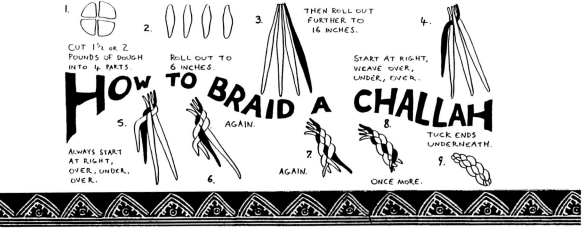

1. CUT 1½ OR 2 POUNDS OF DOUGH INTO 4 PARTS.

2. ROLL OUT TO 6 INCHES.

3. THEN ROLL OUT FURTHER TO 16 INCHES.

4. START AT RIGHT, WEAVE OVER, UNDER, OVER.

HOW TO BRAID A CHALLAH

5. ALWAYS START AT RIGHT, OVER, UNDER, OVER.

6. AGAIN.

7. AGAIN.

8. ONCE MORE.

9. TUCK ENDS UNDERNEATH.

Challah

Yield: 2 loaves

1¼ cup lukewarm water
1 tablespoon yeast
2 eggs
¼ cup oil

⅓ cup sugar
1 teaspoon salt
5½ cups flour

Combine all ingredients except flour. Let stand 15 minutes. Add flour, form a ball and knead for 10 minutes. Place dough in greased bowl and let rise in warm place until doubled, about one hour. Punch dough down and divide into two pieces. Shape into round, long or braided loaves.* Place on greased cookie sheet. Let rise until doubled in size. Brush with egg wash** and sprinkle with poppy or sesame seeds if desired. If loaves are not braided, make several cuts on top with a serrated kinfe. Bake at 350⁰ for 35-40 minutes.

* See previous page for braiding instructions.
**Egg wash is made by beating 1 egg and ½ tablespoons sugar.

Raisin Challah

Yield: 2 loaves

1¼ cup lukewarm water   ⅓ cup sugar

1 tablespoon yeast   1 teaspoon salt

2 eggs   5½ cups flour

¼ cup oil   1 cup raisins

Combine all ingredients except flour. Let stand 15 minutes. Add flour, form a ball and knead for 10 minutes. Add raisins and continue kneading until all raisins are incorporated into the dough. Place dough in greased bowl and let rise in warm place until doubled, about one hour. Punch dough down and divide into two pieces. Shape into round, long or braided loaves.* Place on greased cookie sheet. Let rise until doubled in size. Brush with egg wash** and sprinkle with poppy or sesame seeds if desired. If loaves are not braided, make several cuts on top with a serrated knife. Bake at 350⁰ for 35-40 minutes.

* See preceeding page for braiding instructions.
**Egg wash is made by beating 1 egg and ½ tablespoon sugar.

Corn Rye Bread

Yield: 3 loaves

This recipe was developed similarly to the creation of Los Bagels, due to the absence of any good, locally made Corn Rye. It also comes from dreams of myself as a child eating peanut butter and jelly sandwiches on freshly toasted Corn Rye bread. It was much to my amazement when I discovered that the corn in Corn Rye is traditionally found only on the bottom of the loaf. Many of our older customers from the East coast grew up calling this bread "cornbread" - completely different from what most of us refer to as cornbread i.e. the southern bread made with corn meal.   D.R.

2	cups lukewarm water	5¼	cups high-gluten flour
2	cups rye starter*	4¼	cups white rye flour
1	tablespoon yeast	½	cup caraway seeds
1½	tablespoons salt	½	cup course corn meal
1	tablespoon sugar	1	egg

Mix water, starter, yeast, salt and sugar in a bowl and let set 15 minutes. Add the flours and caraway seeds and knead for 10 minutes. Place dough in greased bowl and let rise in warm place until doubled, about one hour. Punch dough down and divide in three pieces. Form into desired shapes (we sell both long and round loaves). Wet bottom of loaf with water and roll in cornmeal.

Place on baking sheet. Let rise until doubled in size. Brush tops with eggwash (one well beaten egg plus 1 tablespoon water), slash with knife and bake at 350^0 for 40-45 minutes.

*Rye starter is similar to sourdough starter and it gives the bread a tangy and moist consistency. To make your own, combine 4 cups warm water with 4 cups dark rye flour. Mix well, cover and let set 1 or 2 days at room temperature. Take out 2 cups to use for making the corn rye bread and keep remaining starter in a container in a refrigerator. Whenever you want to use the starter, take it out of the refrigerator the night before, add 2 cups dark rye flour and 1-1/2 cups warm water and let set at room temparture overnight. The following morning remove 2 cups to make the bread and return remainder to the refrigerator.

6-Grain Bread

Yield: 2 loaves • Recipe by Martin Mondragon

2	cups warm water	¼	cup sesame seeds
2	tablespoons yeast	¼	cup sunflower seeds
⅓	cup soya oil	1	cup 6 grain mix (9 grain may be substituted)
⅓	cup honey	2	cups high-gluten flour
⅓	cup molasses	4-5	cups whole wheat flour*

*Bread flour may be substituted

Combine all ingredients except flour. Let stand 15 minutes. Add flour, form a ball, knead for 10 minutes. Place dough in greased bowl and let rise in warm place until doubled, about one hour. Punch dough down and divide into two pieces. Flatten pieces, roll up tightly into oblong forms, and place into greased loaf pans. Let rise again until double in size and bake at 350⁰ for 25-30 minutes.

The Illustrator

Steven Vander Meer, was raised in a bakery in Iowa. His family's been baking since the dark ages which is why Steve bakes for us at Los Bagels. He's the 4th generation (it must be hard to avoid). Wonder if the other Vander Meers throw a mean doughball.

As far as we can tell, Steve was run out of town - an altar boy gone bad. At a tender age he discovered shuffling his feet on the carpet would deliver electric shock with the chalice. He doesn't like to talk about his past.

Somehow Steve ended up in Minneapolis pursuing a degree in photography and developing an interest in animated films. After graduating he finished a flick of his own and moved to Humboldt Co. to work on another.

That was 4 or 5 years ago. He got sidetracked doing a couple of commercials. Between bagels and drawings, he works a lot; some call him reclusive. He'll emerge for a game of pool or bowling. Invite him to dinner and he's sure to bring excellent homebrew. He's traded in the slime-green vintage ambulance for a canoe and a mountain bike. He seems content.

Cinnamon Apple Loaf

Yield: 2 loaves
by Steven Vander Meer

As with many of the finest recipes, this one had its' origin as a mistake. Using our challah bread dough and trying to incorporate a mashed up batch of walnuts and raisins (a mixture used as a bagel topping in our deli) this recipe was born. Along with tasting great by itself or with butter it makes outrageous French Toast.

1	cup water (warm)	1	cup raisins
1½	tablespoons yeast	1	cup walnuts
2	eggs	⅓	cup brown sugar
¼	cup oil	2	tablespoons cinnamon
⅓	cup sugar	1½	cups diced apples
2	teaspoons salt		apricot jam
4½-5 cups bread flour			

Dissolve yeast in warm water then add eggs, oil, sugar, salt and mix well. Add flour and knead for 10 minutes. Place dough in a greased bowl and let rise one hour or until double in bulk, set aside. Combine raisins, walnuts, cinnamon and brown sugar (with any broken cookies or chango bars you might have if

you like) in large bowl, set aside. Flatten the dough on a floured table until it's about 1/2" thick. Spread raisin mixture on half of dough, then spread apples over the raisin mixture. Fold the other half of dough over mixture. Then flatten and fold the whole thing twice more. Now here's where the fun begins. With a large knife (cleaver or machete will work) chop the whole thing up into small pieces - very messy but good. Divide pieces into 2 greased 5"x9" loaf pans, let rise 1 hour and they will fuse together. Bake for 1/2 hour at 350^0 then cover with foil and bake 1/2 hour longer.

While still warm remove from pan and brush with glaze. To make glaze mix 1/4 cup water with 1/4 cup apricot-pineapple jam and bring to boil. Remove from heat and brush on warm loaves.

Bolillos

Yield: 1 dozen

A Mexican Roll used as a staple in Mexico and also used to make great "tortas" (i.e. sandwiches). The story goes that when Napoleon invaded Mexico he had the bakers try to duplicate French bread and here's what they got. A great hard roll commonly called "cinco centavo" rolls.

2	cups warm water	1	tablespooon yeast
1	teaspoon salt	3¼	cup high-gluten flour*
1	tablespoon sugar	2	cups bread flour

*White bread flour may be substituted.

For this recipe we use a starter which can be made 1 or 2 days prior to making bolillos. It can also be kept in the refrigerator, but make sure to bring to room temperature before using.

Combine all ingredients except for the high-gluten flour. This is your starter and needs to set at room temperature for a minimum of 12 hours or up to 36 hours. Take the finished starter and add in remaining flour. Knead for 10 minutes. Let rise one hour. Divide dough into 12 pieces. Flatten each piece out, then roll them tightly; put most of the pressure on the ends of the roll so they're pointed at the ends and fat in the middle. Let rise 30 minutes. Make one lengthwise cut 1/2" deep on top of each bolillo and bake at 400° for 22 minutes.

Bread Sculptures for Fun and Profit

With bread dough you can make sculptures to hang on your kitchen wall or to give as unique gifts. Some ideas include alligators, dinosaurs and human figures. Some of the easiest, though, are fish.

Start with one to two pounds of soft dough. (1.) The Challah recipe in this book works very well, but any yeast dough will do. With a rolling pin, flatten the dough to about 3/8 inch thick. (2.) Then, using a dough cutter or serrated knife, cut out a rough shape of what you want to sculpt. (3.) Save all the scraps without wadding them up. Next, round out the edges by cutting off corners, and perhaps cut a mouth. (4.) If you want your creature to be thicker in the middle, put some flat pieces of scrap dough underneath - but not too much. (5.) Now you can use the rest of the scraps to add fins (or legs, claws, horns, antennae . . . whatever).

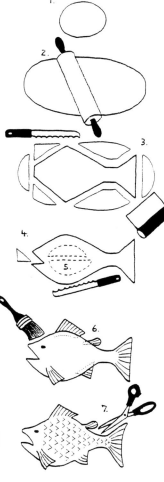

Tuck an edge of the fin under the body of the fish. Then use your finger tips to firmly press down on the seam. (6.) A raisin or nut makes a good eye, and a coating of egg wash gives your sculpture a shiny finish. Egg wash is simply two whole eggs, beaten with one tablespoon of sugar, and applied with a wide paint brush.

Many creatures look better with scales. Add these after the egg wash by holding a pair of scissors at a 45° angle and taking little "snips" at the dough - you don't actually remove any dough. (7.) Try it first on a scrap.

Immediately bake your creature on a cookie sheet at 375° for 25 to 40 minutes, or until a rich, brown color. When its cool, leave it out to thoroughly dry for several days so it won't mold.

Most importantly - use your imagination and have fun!

How J.D. came to be

At 5:30 a.m. John began preparations for a day at the shop. First things being first, he ground 15 lbs. of coffee beans for the day and filled the dispenser. When the days customers filtered in, they began with a mug of that rich steaming brew that animates - coffee. One mug, two mugs, three mugs later and still no satisfying buzz. Must be the fog. But no, unwittingly John had ground 15 lbs. of decaf coffee, unleaded fuel, and not a drop of full strength had been served all day. From that day on John has been known as Johnny Decaf (alias J.D.) throughout Arcata!

John has been with Los Bagels since two weeks after the doors opened. He now heads the wholesale operation.

Chango Bars

One of our best selling sweets. Chango, in Spanish, means monkey man.

½ cup butter
½ cup margarine
2 cups brown sugar
3 eggs
2⅓ cups flour
1 tablespoon baking powder

1 teaspoon salt
1 cup chocolate chips
½ cup mixed nuts
(we roast our own almonds, cashews and sunflower seeds but any combo will do)

Melt butter and margarine. While this is melting cream eggs and brown sugar, then add melted butter and margarine. Combine dry ingredients and mix into sugar mixture. Fold in chocolate chips and nuts. Pour mixture into greased 9"x13" baking pan and bake for 45 - 50 minutes at 350⁰.

WARNING: This batter is deadly delicious and some employees have been known to eat it by the bowl or we've used it as a frosting for cakes.

Double Chocolate Brownies

Recipe by Steven Vander Meer

1¼	cups sugar	¼	cup milk
1	cup butter	1½	cups flour
3	eggs	1	teaspoon salt
4	ozs. unsweetened chocolate	1	teaspoon baking powder
		¾	cup chocolate chips
1	teaspoon vanilla	⅓	cup chopped walnuts

Beat butter and sugar together until creamy. Slowly add in eggs and continue beating. Melt chocolate and add to creamed mixture. Add in milk and vanilla. Combine dry ingredients and mix in. Lastly, add in nuts and chocolate chips. Spread into greased 9"x13" pan and bake for 20 - 25 minutes at 350^0.

Almond Rings

Yield: Approx. 1-1/2 dozen
Recipe by Jodie Harriel

1	cup butter	3¼	cups flour
¾	cup powdered sugar	½	teaspoon salt
1	teaspoon orange extract	½	cup chopped almonds

Cream butter, sugar and orange extract. Add in flour, salt and almonds; mix until forms a ball. Roll dough into a short, fat log. Refrigerate for 2 hours. Slice into rounds approx. 1/4" thick. Bake on ungreased cookie sheet for 16 - 18 minutes at 350⁰.

Variations: Sprinkle powdered sugar on top or dip 1/2 in chocolate.

Bageleros: Where We Come From

timber cruiser. . . university professor. . . winemaker. . . surfer. . .
social worker. . . high school student. . . pastry chef
tofu-maker. . . tire seller. . . mother. . . 4th generation baker. . . hippie . . .
machinist. . . photographer . . . accountant
Philadelphia . . . New Jersey. . . Ohio. . . Whittier. . . Compton . . . Arcata

The people who compose both the past and present Los Bagels are a diverse group indicative of Humboldt County and specifically, Arcata. This small university town is a cultural oasis in the rural coastal area of Northern California. It draws people of different backgrounds and many skills. Los Bagels plumbs that pool to form a stimulating working and social context. As stated in the employee handbook, the intention is "to create a balanced work environment that produces quality products and service, as well as enjoyable, fair and humane working conditions that offer opportunities for personal growth and financial security". The opportunity to grow and journey towards individual hopes and dreams is a benefit one seeks in any experience.

Man Hole Covers

Yield: 1 dozen large cookies
Recipe by Steven Vander Meer

1	cup brown sugar	¾	cup flour
⅔	cup granulated sugar	½	teaspoon salt
½	cup peanut butter	½	teaspoon baking soda
½	cup margarine	1½	cups quick cook oats
2	eggs	6	oz. semi-sweet
1	teaspoon vanilla		chocolate chips

Beat brown sugar, granulated sugar, peanut butter and margarine until fluffy. Cream in eggs and vanilla. Combine dry ingredients, then add to sugar mixture. Lastly add in oatmeal and chocolate chips mixing only until incorporated into batter. With large ice cream scoop, measure out cookies on a lightly greased cookie sheet. We recommend 4 to a cookie sheet. Bake for 16 - 18 minutes at 350⁰.

Bageleros: Where We Are Going (mas o menos)

People come to Los Bagels with their own personal baggage and history. In time, these bageleros depart with a few more possessions (material and intellectual) in pursuit of immediate goals and constantly evolving, often elusive futures. When exploring other countries travelers are usually queried, "Where are you from?" and "Where are you going?" A few bagelero responses to the latter are detailed below.

. . . nurse. . . father. . . college running coach. . . environmental engineer . . . Latin American community development consultant. . . art teacher in Tobago . . . Native American political activist . . . woodworker. . . elementary school teacher. . . restaurant manager. . . on to "the ocean blues" and further.

Mexican Chocolate Crinkles

Yield: 3-4 dozen cookies

1	cup margarine	¼	cup cocoa
1¼	cups sugar	1	teaspoon baking soda
1	egg	½	teaspoon salt
2	tablespoons corn syrup	1	teaspoon cinnamon
1¼	cups flour		

Beat margarine and sugar until creamy then slowly add in the egg and corn syrup. Combine dry ingredients, then add to above mixture and mix in. Drop teaspoons of dough onto lightly greased cookie sheets. Bake 15 minutes at 350⁰.

Rum Pumpkin Bread

Yield: 1 loaf

2¼	cups sugar	1	teaspoon baking powder
4	eggs	½	teaspoon baking soda
1¼	cups oil	¾	teaspoon cloves
2½	cups pumpkin puree (one 16 oz. can)	¾	teaspoon nutmeg
3½	cups flour	1½	teaspoon cinnamon
½	teaspoon salt		

RUM GLAZE

¼	cup water	½	cup sugar
		1	tablespoon rum

Beat together sugar and eggs. Add pumpkin and oil, mix until creamy. In a separate bowl sift together all dry ingredients. Combine dry ingredients with liquid, mix by hand until smooth. Place batter into greased 9"x5" loaf pans. Bake at 350⁰ for 55 minutes.

While bread is still hot, drizzle top with rum glaze. For Glaze: add sugar to water and bring to a boil. Simmer until it thickens, remove from heat, add rum. Drizzle.

Rugalah

Yield: 3 dozen

1	cup butter	½	lb. cream cheese
2¼	cups pastry or cake flour	1	tablespoon vanilla
2	tablespoons powdered sugar	1	egg separated
⅛	teaspoon salt	1½	tablespoons almond extract
		2	tablespoons cinnamon
		¼	cup granulated sugar

RAISIN WALNUT FILLING

1 cup finely chopped walnuts
1 cup raisins

CHOCOLATE WALNUT FILLING

1 cup finely chopped walnuts
1 cup chocolate chips

Combine pastry flour, powdered sugar and salt in food processor. Cut butter into small pieces and add to dry ingredients. Mix until fine crumb consistency. Empty contents into a large bowl, add cream cheese and vanilla. Mix by hand and gather into a ball. Divide dough in 2 pieces. Roll each into a

rectangle 1/4" thick, approx. 8"x18". Brush surfaces with mixture of egg white (slightly beaten) and almond extract. Dust surfaces with cinnamon and sugar mixture. Use your choice of fillings and sprinkle on dough leaving about 1" uncovered. Roll rectangle tightly toward uncovered strip. With egg yolks add 1/4 cup water and beat thoroughly. Brush rolled up pastry with egg wash and cut into 1" pieces. Place on ungreased cookie sheet and bake at 350° for 35 minutes or until golden brown.

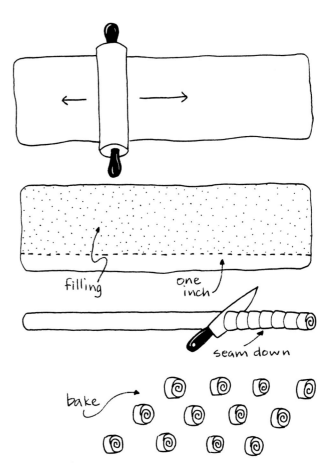

filling

one inch

seam down

bake

Huckleberry Bread

Yield: 1 loaf

2	eggs	1½	teaspoons baking powder
1	egg yolk	½	teaspoon baking soda
½	cup sugar	¼	teaspoon nutmeg
½	cup oil	½	cup + 1 tablespoon milk
1¾	cups flour	1	cup huckleberries
½	teaspoon salt		

Beat together eggs, egg yolk and sugar until creamy. Add oil. Sift together dry ingredients in separate bowl. Add to wet ingredients alternately with milk, mix gently. Add 1 cup huckleberries. Put in lightly greased 9"x5" loaf pan. Bake at 350⁰ for 50 minutes.

Lime Walnut Bread

Yield: 1 loaf

½ cup butter

1 cup sugar

3 eggs

¼ teaspoon almond extract

juice from 2 limes

2 cups flour

½ teaspoon salt

¾ cup chopped walnuts

grated peel of 1 lime

LIME GLAZE

1 tablespoon water

½ cup sugar

juice from 2 limes

grated peel of 1 lime

Cream butter and sugar. Add eggs, lime juice and almond extract, blend well. Fold in flour, salt, walnuts and lime peel. Place batter in 9"x5" loaf pan. Bake at 350⁰ for 55 minutes.

For Lime Glaze: stir together water, lime juice, sugar and lime peel. Bring to a boil, then simmer until it thickens. While bread is still hot, drizzle with lime glaze.

Mandarin Cranberry Bread

Yield: 1 loaf

½	cup butter	½	teaspoon salt
1	cup sugar	½	teaspoon baking soda
1	egg	2	mandarin oranges,
¼	cup milk		peeled & segmented
2	cups flour	6	oz. cranberries
1	teaspoon baking powder		

Cream butter and sugar. Add egg and milk. In a separate bowl sift together dry ingredients. Add to wet mixture gently. Chop up mandarins and cranberries, then stir into the batter. Place into lightly greased 9"x5" loaf pan. This is a very thick batter. Bake at 350° for 50 minutes.

Pumpkin Bran Muffins

Yield: 2 dozen

3   eggs
⅛   cup brown sugar
½   cup pumpkin
     (canned or fresh)
¾   cup oil
¼   cup molasses
½   cup honey
½   cup buttermilk
1   cup whole wheat flour

½   cup white flour
⅔   cup bran
1½   teaspoon baking powder
1½   teaspoon cinnamon
¾   teaspoon baking soda
¾   teaspoon salt
¾   teaspoon nutmeg
¾   teaspoon ginger
½   cup raisins

Place all ingredients in a large bowl. Mix together by hand until completely blended. Divide into muffin tins and bake at 400° for 20-25 minutes.

Blueberry Muffins

Yield: 2 dozen muffins

1	cup margarine	1	tablespoon + 1 teaspoon baking powder
1½	cups sugar		
4	eggs	1	teaspoon salt
1½	cups milk	12	oz. blueberries (fresh or frozen)
3½	cups flour		

Melt margarine in a sauce pan and set aside. Beat together sugar and eggs until creamy. Mix in the milk and melted margarine. Sift together dry ingredients, add them to liquid, gently mixing. Lastly, add blueberries and mix by hand just enough to incorporate. Bake in muffin tins at 400° for 25-30 minutes.

Hanukkah - Chanukah

A very long time ago the Jews in Israel were ruled by the Greeks. They accepted many Greek customs but would not worship Greek gods. Life was tolerable until a new king came along. He insisted that the Jews give up their religion, quit reading the Torah and keeping the Sabbath, or he'd kill them all. The Jews refused.

The king led his huge army from Syria all the way to Jerusalem. They thundered in on elephants, galloped in on horseback, and arrived in waves on foot. Many Jews were killed. But in the mountains a rebel army formed.

The Dreidel

An old custom during Hanukkah is playing games, the most popular being the dreidel. Though the rabbis of the Middle Ages opposed playing games of chance, they permitted it during the long nights of Hanukkah. The dreidel is a top with a different Hebrew letter inscribed on each of its four sides — *nun, gimel, heh, shin*. They form an acronym for the phrase *Neis gadol hayah sham* — "A great miracle happened there." (In Israel the letter *shin* is replaced by a *peh* — "A great miracle happened <u>here</u>.")

Each player has or is given a stake for playing the game. This can be anything from coins (usually pennies) to walnuts. To begin the game, each player puts one coin in the "pot" (if only a few people are playing, they may put two coins in). Then the players take turns spinning the dreidel and following its instructions: The letter *nun* means neither win or lose; *gimel* means you take the whole pot; *heh* means you take half the pot (rounding to the highest number in case of fractions); *shin* means you put one coin in the pot.

Fruit Cake

Yield: 2 pound loaves

Growing up, I always dreaded fruit cake - something really strange about all that fruit in neon like colors. The idea of tons of fruits and nuts in dense bread soaked in brandy sure sounded good to me. Thus the creation of this "non-traditional" fruit cake with no candied fruit — chock full of nuts and dried fruit with a bit of brandy and great flavor. The orange color of dried papaya and green of the pumpkin seeds add to the festive appearance. Give it a try and the holidays may never be the same again.

1	cup dried papaya		¾	cup flour
1	cup dried pineapple		1	cup sugar
1	cup dates		½	teaspoon baking powder
	(we use honey or medjol but any type can be substituted)		2½	cups (8 oz.) chopped almonds
1	cup golden raisins			
⅓	cup brandy		2	cups (6 oz.) chopped walnuts
3	eggs			
1	teaspoon almond extract		2	cups (6 oz.) pumpkin seeds

Dice up all dried fruit and put into a large bowl. Stir eggs, almond extract and half the brandy into the fruit and let stand 1 hour. Combine the rest of the

ingredients and thoroughly mix by hand. Divide evenly into two 4" x 8-1/2" loaf pans. Bake 1 hour 20 minutes at 275°. While still warm, pour remaining brandy over breads to soak in. These breads can be eaten as soon as they cool or tightly wrapped and refrigerated up to several months. Many folks like to periodically soak them with brandy if they are to be stored for a long period of time. This is not necessary but does enhance the flavor.

Mexican Chocolate Pie

Yield: (1) 9" pie

CRUST

1	cup raw almonds	¾	cup flour
¼	cup sugar	½	cup butter
¼	cup brown sugar		

Chop almonds very fine, a food processor works best. Combine almonds with dry ingredients, then cut butter in small pieces and blend everything in food processor. Press dough evenly into 9" ungreased pie pan. Bake 12 - 15 minutes at 400⁰ or until center turns brown. Cool.

FILLING

2½	oz. chocolate chips (a heaping 1/3 cup)	2	eggs
½	cup butter softened	1	teaspoon cinnamon
¾	cup powdered sugar	1	teaspoon almond extract

Melt chocolate. Combine butter, powdered sugar, cinnamon and almond extract. Beat until smooth and creamy. Add chocolate. Blend well. Add eggs

one at a time, beat until thoroughly blended and fluffy, scraping the sides of the bowl frequently.

Put filling into baked pie crust and top with toasted sliced almonds (optional). Refrigerate several hours. Pie may be topped with whipped cream and chocolate shavings after refrigerating.

New York Style Cheesecake

Yield: (1) 10" cheesecake
Recipe by Martin Mondragon

2½	lbs. cream cheese	3	eggs plus 2 yolks
1½	cups sugar	¾	cup milk
2½	tablespoons cornstarch	½	tablespoon vanilla

In a large bowl cream the cream cheese. In a smaller bowl mix together sugar and cornstarch then slowly add to cream cheese. Next add eggs one at a time then add the milk and vanilla. Grease a 10" cake or springform pan and line bottom with wax paper. Pour batter into pan and bake in a water bath in the oven for 1 hour 20 minutes at 350°. Always keep water in bath to prevent curdling. Cool and remove from pan.

We make this cheesecake with a 1/2" slice of Chocolate layer cake on the bottom. This isn't necessary but adds a nice touch to this recipe. Any chocolate layer cake may be used.

Passover / Pesach

Pesach, meaning "passover", is celebrated every year in spring. Festivities revolve around a feast, the Seder, during which the story of the Exodus is told. Everyone participates by chanting, playing games and reading the Haggadah. Passover's lesson is that the Exodus not be forgotten, so the emphasis is on teaching children.

The story is illustrated with symbolic foods. Roasted egg represents ancient festival offerings. A paste of walnuts, wine and apple symbolizes the bricks Jews made as slaves when building cities for the Pharaoh. There are bitter herbs and saltwater to recall the hardships and tears of captivity. Roasted lamb reminds everyone of the lambs' blood which Jews used to mark their doors signaling God's Angel of Death to passover their homes. God's curse killed the Egyptians first born sons, thus the Pharaoh relented and let the Jews go free.

At the Seder, three whole matzohs represent the three tribes of the Jews. Only unleavened bread is consumed during Pesach to commemorate how the Jews fled in haste and had to bake their bread in the desert without yeast. Sweet herbs are part of the meal too, symbolizing liberation.

Throughout the Seder toasts are made and a glass is filled for the prophet Elijah. On this imporant holiday, his presence is essential; he is prophet of hope.

Poppy Seed Muffins

Yield: 2 dozen • Recipe by Jodie Harriel

1	cup margarine	1½	cups buttermilk
1	cup brown sugar	3	cups flour
1	cup granulated sugar	¾	teaspoon baking powder
3	eggs	¾	teaspoon baking soda
2	teaspoons vanilla	¾	teaspoon salt
⅓	cup coffee	⅓	cup poppy seeds

TOPPING

¾	cup brown sugar	1½	tablespoons butter
1½	tablespoons flour	¾	cup chopped walnuts
2	teaspoons cinnamon		

Combine brown sugar, white sugar and eggs and mix until smooth. Add coffee, vanilla, buttermilk. Add melted margarine and continue mixing. Combine and add remaining dry ingredients. Divide into muffin tins.

For topping, combine softened butter with brown sugar, cinnamon and flour and mix until finely crumbed, add walnuts. Sprinkle mixture onto muffins, then bake at 400° for 20-25 minutes.

Oat Bran Muffins

Yield: 1-1/2 dozen
Recipe by Martin Mondragon

⅔ cup oil

1½ cups milk

½ cup honey

⅓ cup concentrated
apple juice

¾ cup crushed pineapple

½ cup brown sugar

1⅔ cups bread flour

¾ cup whole wheat flour

¾ cup oat bran

2¼ cups bran

1 tablespoon baking soda

1 tablespoon baking powder

¼ teaspoon salt

½ cup chopped dates
oatmeal

Combine all ingredients in a large bowl, mix well. Divide batter into muffin tins, sprinkle tops with oatmeal. Bake 20 - 25 minutes at 400⁰.

Empanadas

Yield: 2-1/2 dozen

Most Latin American countries have some version of empanadas or "turnovers" filled with a variety of fruits, meats and vegetables. Depending upon the area, they are either baked or fried. As a kid I have fond memories of going to the Panaderia near my grandparents house and getting empanadas de calabasa or pumpkin empanadas. Our two fillings are the traditional Mexican pumpkin filling and another we developed at Los Bagels, green chile and potato. Both are great served warm or cold.

MARTIN'S SISTER'S FLAKY DOUGH

3³/₄-4 cups flour	1¼ cups cold water
1 tablespoon sugar	1 egg
1 teaspoon salt	³/₄ tablespoon white vinegar
1 cup + 1 tablespoon butter or shortening	Filling of choice

Fillings on next page

Empanada Fillings

PUMPKIN

1   can pumpkin (1lb.12 oz.)

⅛   teaspoon ground cardamon

2   teaspoons cinnamon

¼   teaspoon vanilla

2   tablespoons melted butter

½   cup brown sugar

GREEN CHILE & POTATO

1   medium onion chopped

2   tablespoons minced garlic

⅓   cup olive oil

2   cups chopped green chile

3   medium diced potatoes

½   teaspoon salt

1   bunch cilantro

With a pastry cutter or fork, mix flour, sugar, salt and margarine until it resembles pea sized grains. Whisk together water, egg and vinegar and add to dry ingredients. Roll out dough on floured board to 1/8" thick and cut into 5" or 4" diameter circles (use a can or jar lid). Fill with 1-2 tablespoons of desired filling. Moisten edges around dough, fold in half and press with a fork to seal edges. Brush with a mixture of 2 eggs and 1 tablespoon sugar. Make 1" slit on each empanada and put on greased cookie sheet. Bake 25 minutes at 375⁰ or until golden brown.

To make the pumpkin filling combine all the ingredients and mix for 2 - 3 minutes.

For the green chile filling, saute onion and garlic in olive oil until the onions are slightly brown and remove from heat. Add potatoes, cilantro, green chile and salt to onion mixture. Each filling recipe is enough for 2-1/2 dozen empanadas.

Knish Dough

4	cups all-purpose flour	³⁄₄	teaspoon lemon juice
2	cups pastry flour	2 ⅛	cup cold water
³⁄₄	teaspoon salt	3 ½	sticks cold butter

    In a large mixing bowl combine both flours with lemon juice, water and salt. Mix by hand until the dough is smooth. (5 to 10 minutes) Next put it on a wax paper on a bake pan. Flatten by hand into a rectangle 1/2" thick. Refrigerate for two hours.

    The dough and the butter must be the same consistency/firmness when you take them out. When the dough is ready, put it on a floured surface, roll out to 8" x 16" x 1/4" thick. Slice butter 1/4" thick and layer on one half of the dough leaving 1/2" margins around the edges. (fig. 1) Fold other halve over the buttered half and crimp under the edges to seal the butter inside. (fig. 2) Roll out to 1/2" thick (fig. 3) Now start the process of making a book fold. Fold in the ends so they just meet making a piece of dough roughly square. (fig. 4) Then fold over in half to create the rectangular form in figure 5. Turn this piece at a right angle and roll it out to 1/2" thick - 8" x 16" rectangle and make the book fold one more time. This time stop when you have dough in shape of figure 5. Wrap this in plastic wrap and let rest in the refrigerator over night.

    Next day roll out and make book folds two more times - again stop at

the shape in figure 5 and store over night under refrigeration.

On the third day roll out to 12" x 24" (fig. 7) (should be close to 1/8" thick). With a pizza cutter make 4" x 4" squares (fig. 8). You should end up with 18 of them. Each square gets 1/4 cup of filling heaped in the center. (fig. 9) To fold, bring opposite corners together. (fig.10) Now do the same with the other two corners. (fig 11) It's important to fasten these corners by overlapping and make sure that filling can't escape. Make pucker in the very middle. (fig. 12) Be careful not to stretch the dough too tightly, again you are making sure the filling doesn't escape. Flip over the finished knish, place on a baking pan (lined with baking parchment makes clean up easier). Leave at least 3" around each one. Flatten the knish to 1" thick (fig. 13) Brush the top with an egg wash made from a egg beaten with 2 teaspoons of tap water. (fig. 14)

Bake at 375^0 for 45 minutes or until they are golden brown on top and slightly brown on the bottom.

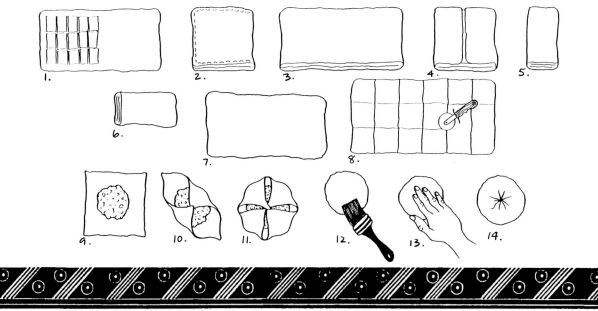

Potato Knish Filling

yields 18 - 1/4 cup portions

3 ¾ cups cooked
mashed potatoes
¾ cup shredded carrots
¼ cup diced green onions

1½ tablespoon melted butter
⅓ teaspoon salt
¼ teaspoon pepper

Mix ingredients thoroughly.

Corn-Green Chile Filling

yields 18 - 1/4 cup portions

2 ½ cups cooked
mashed potatoes
½ cup chopped green chilies
1 cup drained canned corn

1½ cup grated
cheddar cheese
1 teaspoon salt
¾ cup sugar

Allow potatoes to cool before adding other ingredients. Mix thoroughly.

Kuchen

2   cups margarine
2   cups sugar
4   eggs
4   cups flour
4   teaspoons baking powder
Enough fresh fruit halves to cover batter

Cream margarine and sugar together until the mixture is smooth then add eggs continuing to mix until thoroughly blended.

Combine the dry ingredients and mix them into the creamed ingredients. Spread batter in an 11"x18" baking sheet. Arrange fruit halves on top and sprinkle them with cinnamon sugar. Bake for 50 to 55 minutes at 350°.

Cut into squares to serve.

Soups, Spreads & Chile Verde

Las Posadas

Las Posadas, a Mexican Christmas tradition, is a re-enactment of Mary and Joseph's search for lodging. Guests at a posada meet outside the host's home with candles and figures of the Virgin Mary, Joseph and an angel. People gather at the door singing, and request entrance to the home of their host. After the singing, they are invited in and kneel at the Nativity scene.

The festivities of the evening include a supper of chicken or turkey mole. Mole is a special sauce of chile, chocolate and other spices. There is also a pinata - a clay jar covered in paper mache' which is shaped as an animal and is covered in colored paper. Inside the pinata are toys, candies and tiny gifts. A child is blindfolded and swings a stick attempting to break the pinata and get the prizes out. The breaking of the pinata usually causes the kids to scramble for the prizes that come raining down.

Pesto Spread

Yield: 2 -3 cups

*½ cup chopped basil
    (tightly packed)
¼ cup walnuts
2 cloves garlic

3 tablespoons olive oil
1 lb. cream cheese
¼ cup milk
1 teaspoon salt

In a food processor, blend basil, walnuts, garlic and oil and set aside. Next blend remaining ingredients until creamy, then add walnut basil mixture.

*Basil can be frozen during its season and used throughout the year. We blend up fresh basil and pack it in 8 oz. containers to use throughout the year.

Hummus

Yield: Approx 2 cups

1   can (15 oz.)
    garbanzo beans
2   tablespoons Tahini
    (roasted)
¼   medium onion
1   clove garlic

½   tablespoon lemon juice
2   teaspoons soy sauce
¼   teaspoon cayenne
2   tablespoons chopped
    cilantro

Drain garbanzo beans - reserve liquid. In food processor (blender will work) blend all ingredients until smooth, slowly adding 1-2 tablespoons of liquid from beans to make a smooth spreadable consistency.

Sopa de Maiz (Corn Soup)

Yield: 3 quarts

2	tablespoons butter		½	cup chopped tomatoes
½	cup chopped onions		½	teaspoon oregano
4	cloves garlic		1	tablespoon salt
¾	cup chopped celery		½	teaspoon cumin
1½	qts. water		½	tablespoon chile powder
2	cups fresh corn		1	cup milk
	(canned or frozen may be substituted)		¼	cup flour
1	can (3½ oz.) Ortega green chiles		⅛	cup chopped parsley
			¾	cup grated jack cheese

Saute onion, garlic and celery in butter for 10 - 15 minutes. Add water, corn, chile, tomatoes and spices. Bring to a boil then turn down, and simmer 15 minutes. In a small bowl slowly mix milk into the flour until smooth. Add to soup, stirring continuously. Cook for 15 minutes longer, then add cheese and parsley before serving.

Day of the Dead / Dia de los Muertos

Dia de los Muertos is a national festival in Mexico observing the Day of the Dead. It's a fun holiday. Bakeries sell Pan de Muerto (Bread of the Dead) shaped like skulls and crossbones, candy shops sell candy skulls and skeletons, and toy shops sell skull masks and cardboard skeletons that pop out of cardboard coffins. Around midnight the night before, Mexicans begin assembling the gifts, food and candles they will take to their relatives' gravesites. They believe these souls are permitted a visit at 3:00 in the afternoon on November 2nd.

On the Day of the Dead people spread mats on the ground and set up wooden frames decorated with marigolds and fruit to welcome spirits. Incense is burned and candles are lit for every one remembered. The ghosts warm themselves over the flames, partake of the offerings and rest after their long journey. Ultimately, it's the living who consume the provisions while celebrating in each other's homes.

16 de Septiembre / Cinco de Mayo

These two days are celebrated as Mexican Independence days. On the 16th of September in 1810, Father Miguel Hidalgo rang the town church bell summoning people to fight for their independence for the Gauchupines (Spaniards). His call to arms, the famous Grito de Dolores, or Cry from Dolores, proclaimed loyalty to the Virgin of Guadalupe and vowed freedom from tyranny.

Cinco de Mayo (5th of May) celebrates the first major defeat of the French, in 1862, who were occupying Mexico. This decisive victory was led by General Porfirio Diaz on May 5th, 1862, and represents Mexican solidarity today. It is odd that Americans think of Cinco de Mayo as _the_ day of Mexican Independence where as Mexicans, who celebrate both days, consider the 16th de Septiembre more important.

Indonesian Peanut Celery Soup

Yield: 4 quarts

1½	cups chopped celery	1	fresh Serrano chile-diced
½	cup chopped onion	1	teaspoon salt
4	tablespoons butter	1	can (12 oz.) coconut milk
3	cloves minced garlic	⅔	cup unsalted roasted peanuts
2	qts. water	¼	cup flour
1	lb. crunchy peanut butter	¼	cup milk
2	teaspoons curry powder		

Chop up celery, onion, garlic, saute in butter for 10 minutes. Add water, peanut butter and spices. Bring to a boil then turn down to simmer. Add coconut milk. In a small bowl slowly mix milk into the flour until a heavy cream consistency. Slowly add to soup stirring constantly. Continue stirring for 15 - 20 minutes as soup thickens. Just before serving add peanuts.

Lox or Smoked Salmon

Each is a delicacy made from Salmon which has first been cured, and then smoked. The difference lies in the method of smoking.

What we in the West call lox is smoked at 80^0. In the East they call it "Scotia" or Nova Scotian-style smoked salmon. This temperature protects the nature of the flesh so that it's very moist and sliceable.

"Smoked Salmon" on the other hand must be smoked at 140^0 further dehydrating the fish and rendering the flesh flaky. Indians invented this method as a way to preserve their catch; it does last longer without refrigeration. Back East they might call this style "kippered" or "hard-smoked salmon."

At Los Bagels we serve the cold-smoked salmon as lox, and the hard-smoked we call smoked salmon. In our part of the Northwest, both varieties seem to be equally appreciated, although most folks are more familiar with hard smoked salmon.

Lox Spread

Yield: 2 -3 cups

2	green onions	½	cup milk
½	lb. lox or lox trim	1	lb. cream cheese
1	clove garlic		

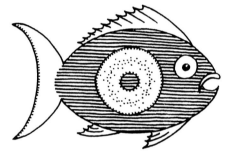

First blend softened cream cheese with milk until smooth. Finely chop green onion and add to cream cheese mixture. Put garlic through garlic press and add. Add coarsely chopped or broken up lox or lox trim.

Mix in food processor only enough to thoroughly mix still leaving small pieces of lox throughout the spread.

Chile Verde de mi Tía María

Yield: Serves 4

1½	lbs. pork shoulder or venison	6-8	N. Mexico green chile or 2 small cans green chile
1	medium onion	3	tablespoons flour
2	medium tomatoes	1-1½	qts. hot water
3	cloves garlic		salt

Cut up pork into small pieces. Heat oil in large frying pan or Dutch oven. When hot, add pork and brown. Mince the garlic and add to the pork while cooking. Pork takes about 10 - 15 minutes. Dice up onion and tomatoes and shred chile with your hands. When pork is browned, turn up heat to full and add flour. Stir continually to brown the flour. Slowly add 1 qt. hot water and stir. Immediately turn down to simmer, add onions, tomatoes and chile. Simmer for 1/2 hour or longer - add water if necessary. Should be a thin consistency. Salt to taste.¡Bien Provecho!

Brazilian Black Bean Soup

Yield: 4 quarts

4	cups black beans	1½	tablespoons salt
¼	cup olive oil	1	cup sliced carrots
4	cloves minced garlic	¾	cup chopped celery
1	cup chopped onion		cilantro
2	tablespoons chile powder		sour cream
1	tablespoon cumin		

Sort through beans getting rid of any rocks, or rotten beans. Cover with water and soak overnight. After soaking, make sure beans are covered with water. Bring to boil and turn down to simmer. In a separate pan saute onions and garlic in oil, then add to beans. Next add the carrots, celery and spices. Simmer 2 - 3 hours until beans are done. Soup may be garnished with fresh cilantro and sour cream.

Guacamole

Yield: Serves 4-6

2   ripe avocados - preferably Hass or Fuerte

1   tablespoon Jalapeños- chopped

1   clove garlic

juice from 1 lemon or 2 limes

1-2   teaspoons salt

½   medium diced onion

1   medium tomato diced

¼   bunch fresh cilantro

Peel and mash avocados. Finely chop jalapeños and garlic and add to avocados along with juice from lime or lemon. Dice onion, tomato and cilantro. Add to mixture and salt to taste. ¡Bien Provecho!

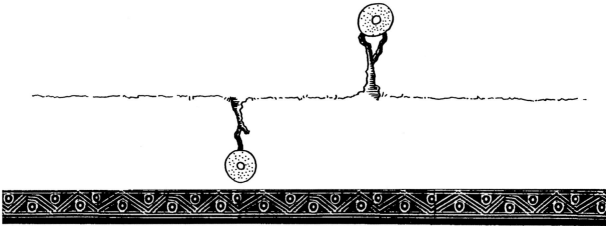

For Here or To Go?

Los Bagels T-shirts

All shirts are 3 color available in black

Long sleeve (size XL, L, M, SM)	$14.00
Short Sleeve	$12.50
Tanks (S, M, L)	$12.50
Kids	$8.50
Closed Tuesdays (size XL, L, l. slv teal only)	$14.00

Los Bagels Logo Mug $8.00

Black 16 oz. ceramic Mug with 3 color logo

Recipes and Lore $14.95

Los Bagels cookbook filled with all the recipes and lore which makes Los Bagels what it is.

Travel Mug $5.60

For Bageleros on the go!

Bagels
Call for price - orders vary depending on variety and location.

All varieties available include onion, garlic, poppy, sesame, salt, whole wheat & raisin, jalapeno, pumpernickel and slugs.

Prices subject to change • All bagel orders to be shipped Federal Express overnight.

82

ORDER FORM

1061 "I" Street • Arcata, CA • 95521 • (707) 822-3150
403 2nd Street • Eureka, CA • (707) 442-8525

Qty.	Description (include size, color ,flavor)	Price Ea.	Total

— All orders include shipping and handling except for bagels. Please call for pricing.

Subtotal _____
CA res. add 7.25% tax _____
TOTAL _____

Name _____

Street _____

City _____ State _____ Zip_____

Phone hm._____ wk. _____

ORDER FORM

1061 "I" Street • Arcata, CA • 95521 • (707) 822-3150
403 2nd Street • Eureka, CA • (707) 442-8525

Qty.	Description (include size, color ,flavor)	Price Ea.	Total

— All orders include shipping and handling except for bagels. Please call for pricing.

Subtotal _____
CA res. add 7.25% tax _____
TOTAL _____

Name _____

Street _____

City _____ State _____ Zip_____

Phone hm._____ wk. _____